FEDERAL ACCOUNTING STANDARDS ADVISORY BOARD

RULES OF PROCEDURE

UPDATED OCTOBER 2010

TABLE OF CONTENTS

RULES OF PROCEDURE

AMENDED AND RESTATED THROUGH OCTOBER 2010

INTRODUCTION

The Federal Accounting Standards Advisory Board (FASAB, "the Board") was created under the terms of the Federal Advisory Committee Act (FACA), as amended, (5 U.S.C. app.) and is sponsored by the Comptroller General of the United States, the Director of the Office of Management and Budget (OMB), and the Secretary of the Treasury of the United States.

The Sponsors established the Board by Memorandum of Understanding (MOU) dated October 10, 1990, and have amended the MOU periodically since then to enhance the FASAB's structure and operations.[1] In addition, since 1999, FASAB has been the body designated by the American Institute of Certified Public Accountants (AICPA) to establish generally accepted accounting principles (GAAP) for federal government reporting entities.[2]

The MOU addresses:

1. the fundamental purpose of the Board,
2. Board composition,
3. member selection and appointment process,
4. tenure of members,
5. duties of the Board,
6. administrative guidelines and management controls, and
7. a six-step process for considering accounting standards.

The MOU's six-step process is:

1. identification of accounting issues and agenda decisions,
2. preliminary deliberations,
3. preparation of initial documents (issues papers and/or discussion memorandums),

---

[1]Subsequent to FASAB's creation by its sponsors, Congress specifically recognized FASAB in several laws, including section 802(a)(6) of the Federal Financial Management Improvement Act of 1996 (31 U.S.C. § 3512 note), the Department of the Interior and Related Agencies Appropriations Act, 1999 (Pub. L. No. 105-277, div. A, § 101(e)), and annual government-wide appropriations act provisions, such as section 722 of the Financial Services and General Government Appropriations Act, 2010 (Pub. L. No. 111-117, div. C, title VII).

[2]AICPA Code of Professional Conduct, ET § 203.03 (http://www.aicpa.org/about/code/et_203.html#et_203.01).

4. release of preliminary documents to the public, public hearings, and considerations of comments,
5. further deliberations, exposure draft, and consideration of comments, and
6. at least a two-thirds majority vote reached among the members in favor of concepts and standards submitted to the Comptroller General, the Secretary of the Treasury, and the Director of OMB.[3]

The MOU provides that the Board will determine the detailed procedures necessary to implement this six-step process. In addition to implementing the MOU, the Board relies on these rules of procedure to ensure continued conformance with the AICPA's criteria for bodies it designates as the source for GAAP. These criteria are:

1. **Independence** - The body should be independent from the undue influence of its constituency.

2. **Due Process and Standards** – The body should follow a due process that is documented and open to all relevant aspects or alternatives. The body's aim should be to produce standards that are timely and that provide for full, fair, and comparable disclosure.

3. **Domain and Authority** - The body should have a unique constituency not served by another existing Rule 203 standard-setting body. Its standards should be generally accepted by its constituencies.

4. **Human and Financial Resources** - The body should have sufficient funds to support its work. Its members and staff should be highly knowledgeable in all relevant areas.

5. **Comprehensiveness and Consistency** - The body should approach its processes comprehensively and follow concepts consistent with those of existing Rule 203 standard-setting bodies for analogous circumstances.

These rules of procedure are designed to:

1. implement the six-step process provided in the MOU,
2. support continued conformance with the criteria for a GAAP standard-setting body specified by the AICPA,
3. provide a means for the public and the profession to monitor the performance of FASAB relative to the established criteria,
4. achieve the performance improvement objectives of the Government Performance and Results Act of 2003, and

---

[3] The MOU provides a specific requirement for Statements of Federal Financial Accounting Standards and Concepts. The rules adopted in this document present the specific requirements for approval or publication of a variety of documents. Where a voting requirement is governed by a document other than these rules a reference to and a summary of the requirement is provided.

5. ensure timely notification of both the Sponsors and the profession should performance diminish significantly.

As such, these rules of procedure are intended to permit timely, thorough, and open study of federal accounting issues and encourage public participation in the process of improving federal accounting concepts and standards. Open study assures that federal accounting concepts and standards are well-considered and designed to advance the public interest. Individuals and organizations are invited to make their views known to the FASAB through thoughtful, reasoned, and timely communication at all stages in the FASAB's processes.

GENERAL PROCEDURES

The general procedures used by the Board during the six-step process provided in the MOU are described in the sections that follow. In addition, greater detail is provided in Appendices. Appendix A, *Resources*, describes the roles of the Chairperson, the Executive Director, the staff, task forces, the Administrative Steering Committee, the Appointments Panel, and fellows. Appendix B, *Notices, Meetings, and Public Hearings*, describes the requirements for public notices, meetings, and hearings; including requirements of the FACA. Note that all meetings, publications, and records of FASAB are subject to notice and access requirements of the FACA. These requirements are not separately identified in the general procedures provided below. Appendix C, *Publications,* describes the various types of FASAB publications used, member options for alternative views and dissents, and specific due process requirements followed for each type. Appendix D, *Media Relations Policy*, provides the Board's policy and offers guidelines for dealing with members of the press.

1. IDENTIFY ACCOUNTING ISSUES AND DECIDE ON AGENDA ITEMS

The FASAB consults with the Executive Director to prioritize its potential projects. New projects are added to the active agenda based on periodic prioritization by the Board. The Executive Director ensures that agenda decisions are initiated in advance of staff becoming available to take on new work so that pre-agenda research will be conducted. All agenda decisions are made at meetings of the FASAB by oral polling with agreement of at least a majority of members polled required for approval.

To prepare for the FASAB consultation, the Executive Director solicits timely suggestions from other individuals and organizations. The Executive Director, after consultation with the Chairperson, may publish brief descriptions of potential projects and request input from selected individuals and groups on the potential projects and other emerging issues. In addition, the Chairperson may decide to convene an agenda hearing to discuss potential projects with stakeholders. For information on notice and meeting requirements, see Appendix B.

In addition to agenda setting initiated by FASAB, any individual or organization may request in writing or at an open meeting that the FASAB address a new issue, or review or reexamine any effective Statement of Federal Financial Accounting Standards, Statement of Federal Financial Accounting Concepts, or other effective provision of federal accounting principles. The FASAB will respond to such communications and explain its disposition of the request.

2. CONDUCT PRELIMINARY DELIBERATIONS

The FASAB deliberates on active agenda items at its meetings. Through the deliberative process, the FASAB ensures that all issues are identified; alternatives for resolving issues are developed, assessed, and ranked; public solicitation of comments is appropriate; and explanations for the final decisions are provided.

During preliminary deliberations, members are asked to express their preferences among alternatives. Based on these expressions of preference as well as members' requests for additional research, progress is made toward preparation of preliminary documents and/or exposure drafts. Initial (deliberative) documents are provided to the Board to facilitate preliminary deliberations.

3. PREPARE INITIAL DOCUMENTS

FASAB deliberations are facilitated by initial (deliberative) documents that provide:

a) background information including current accounting and reporting practices, relevant federal concepts and standards, laws and regulations, and budgetary information needs or concerns;

b) summaries of concepts/standards promulgated or being developed by other standard setters in other domains; and/or

c) an initial listing of options including pros/cons and illustrations where possible.

The Executive Director provides initial documents to members in advance of meetings. Initial documents may be prepared by staff, task forces appointed by the Chairperson, individual members, or other experts and organizations.

4. RELEASE PRELIMINARY DOCUMENTS, CONVENE PUBLIC HEARINGS, AND CONSIDER COMMENTS

The FASAB may release preliminary documents, consistent with the requirements of FACA, related to federal accounting and financial reporting. These documents are preliminary to exposure drafts communicating formal proposals of the Board for public comment. The Board is not required to issue preliminary documents before developing and issuing an exposure draft.

Preliminary documents include, among others, research reports, discussion memorandums, invitations to comment, preliminary views, summary and related documents, responses to requests and inquiries, and statements of policy dealing with matters of federal accounting and financial reporting.

Text of the preliminary documents include (1) attribution, (2) explanation of the nature of the publication, (3) relevant research material, and (4) directions for submitting comments if requested. Preliminary documents may be attributed to (1) the Board, (2) staff, (3) a task force, or (4) others conducting research on behalf of the Board. If documents are attributed to the Board, the Board is expressing its views or identifying alternatives it believes are viable. For documents not attributed to the Board, a disclaimer should be presented in addition to attribution.

In addition to initial documents for the Board's use, task forces or the staff may prepare either research reports or discussion memorandums for publication. Research reports (RR) and discussion memorandums (DM) provide research findings and relevant literature. DMs include alternative solutions to the issues under consideration, present the known implications and arguments regarding each, and request comments. RRs also may include alternative solutions but do not request comments. Task force and staff prepared preliminary documents may be issued upon approval by the

Chairperson. The Chairperson confers with the Board prior to deciding whether to issue individual DMs and RRs.

The Board may publish invitations to comment (ITC) or preliminary views (PV). Both ITCs and PVs request comments. ITCs present issues that might be addressed by the Board in the future or alternative solutions to issues under consideration. PVs present the Board's preliminary selection of a solution, although alternative solutions may be presented. Summary or other documents related to ITCs or PVs also may be published. ITCs, PVs and related summary or other documents will only be issued after at least a majority vote of the Board approving the publication. See section 6, Vote, for voting requirements.

The Board also may issue responses to requests and inquiries, and statements of policy. The Chairperson may issue these documents under his signature at his discretion. In addition, the Chairperson may delegate this authority to the Executive Director.

For any preliminary documents soliciting comments (e.g., discussion memorandum, invitation to comment, or preliminary views), the Board members receive all comments as well as a staff summary. The staff summary and accompanying analysis address all comments and identify issues requiring consideration.

In addition to considering the written responses, summary, and staff analysis, the Board may elect to convene a public hearing. The public hearing permits the Board and staff to ask questions about information and points of view submitted by respondents. The Board will announce its intent to convene a public hearing consistent with the notice requirements in Appendix B.

5. CONDUCT FURTHER DELIBERATIONS, RELEASE EXPOSURE DRAFT, AND CONSIDER COMMENTS

The Board will continue its deliberations and may (a) receive additional initial documents, (b) prepare other preliminary documents, (c) begin developing an exposure draft, or (d) defer the project. If an exposure draft is developed, it will:

a) specify what type of final pronouncement (e.g., a statement of federal financial accounting standard, interpretation) is proposed,
b) request comments by a certain date and provide instructions for submission (see Appendix C, *Publications* for minimum comment periods for different types of final publications),
c) either announce the date of the planned public hearing or explain that the Board may decide[4] to convene a public hearing after considering comments,
d) list specific questions that the Board wishes respondents to address,

---

[4] Majority approval is required to convene a public hearing.

e) present a summary and complete proposed pronouncement,

f) propose an effective date, and

g) explain the basis for the proposed conclusions and present any alternative views expressed by members.

Exposure drafts of Statements of Federal Financial Accounting Standards or Concepts (SFFAS or SFFAC, or "Statements") and interpretations are issued only after at least a majority vote of the Board. See Appendix C, *Publications*, for content specifications, and due process procedures. See section 6 below for voting requirements.

Following the exposure period, the Board considers responses, convenes a public hearing as appropriate,[5] and deliberates on issues and options identified by respondents.

The Board may continue its deliberations based on these responses, and any public hearing input, and may (a) request and consider additional initial documents, (b) elect to issue another exposure draft (sometimes referred to as re-exposure), (c) defer the project, or (d) proceed with development of a final pronouncement.

If the Board elects to proceed to a final pronouncement, it makes necessary but not substantive revisions to the proposals in the exposure draft and prepares any required content for the final pronouncement. See Appendix C for required content of each type of final pronouncement. Appendix C also provides direction for inclusion of member dissents in final pronouncements.

---

[5] Public hearings, while not required, are preferred.

6. VOTE

The FASAB will not issue any preliminary document, exposure draft or final pronouncement, or other document in which the Board takes a position on accounting issues without the approval of members as specified in the MOU or these rules of procedure. Publications that do not establish a Board position – Technical Releases of the Accounting and Auditing Policy Committee or Technical Bulletins issued by FASAB staff – are issued if a majority of members do not object.

Following are detailed provisions regarding voting:

1) <u>Eligibility to vote</u>. Only the members are eligible to vote; no substitutes may be designated. Unless s/he abstains, a member of the FASAB may vote even if s/he was not a member or for some other reason did not participate during the research, discussion, or deliberative periods. A FASAB member may continue to participate in public hearings and other meetings during the research, discussion, and deliberative periods even though s/he plans to abstain on a particular vote.

2) <u>Quorum</u>. A majority of FASAB members serving on the Board constitutes a quorum necessary for a meeting to be held.

3) <u>Board Approval</u>. The agreement of at least a majority of FASAB members voting is required to approve all matters. For issuance of a Statement the agreement of at least a two-thirds majority is required by the MOU. (See Appendix C: Publications for information regarding the approval process for each type of publication.) For all other matters, at least a simple majority is required. In the case of vacancy, the approval of at least a majority or two-thirds majority of the remaining members of the FASAB voting is necessary for approval.

4) <u>Ballots</u>.
   a) <u>Form</u>. Where any action of the FASAB requires a vote of its members, such vote is by written ballot of its members. Ballots may be via electronic means. In this case, the electronic ballots returned by members serve as written ballots.
   b) <u>Record-keeping</u>. Votes of each Board member regarding the publication of any document shall be retained as part of the public file of the FASAB, including any dissents by individual Board members.
   c) <u>Timing</u>. The Chairman will poll the Board members on most issues at a meeting of the Board. Members' oral expressions of views constitute a "sense of the Board" but are not votes. Following oral approval at a meeting, the Executive Director will arrange for written ballots to be conveyed to members along with a final draft of the document. Written ballots will indicate a due date for votes. Generally, due dates will afford the members at least 10 working days to consider the ballot. Any member not submitting a vote within four working days after the deadline will be considered to have abstained. The Chairperson may determine that a later or earlier due date is warranted after consulting with the Board members regarding the urgency of the matter and their own availability to address the matter. The Chairperson will notify

members of the due date including the date by which a member not submitting a vote will be considered to have abstained.

5) <u>Dissents</u>. Individual members may offer dissents to any final pronouncement (e.g, documents other than an exposure draft or a preliminary document). Any dissents shall be published as part of the final pronouncement. Generally, dissents include not only the fact that the member objects to the pronouncement but also an explanation of the member's reason for objecting. The minutes and the publications shall include the name of any member who dissents to a pronouncement or abstains from voting.

6) <u>Alternative Views</u>. Individual members may offer alternative views on an exposure draft or a preliminary document. Any alternative views will be published in the document and should solicit input from respondents. Alternative views will identify the name(s) of the member(s) expressing that view. The minutes shall include the name of any member who opposes any exposure draft or preliminary document, proposes an alternative view, or abstains from voting.

ISSUANCE OF FINAL PRONOUNCEMENTS

Final pronouncements are issued by FASAB only after compliance with the procedures specified in the MOU and in these rules of procedure. For ease of reference, these procedures are summarized in Appendix C, *Publications*. In addition, public notice requirements of the FACA apply.

APPENDIX A: RESOURCES

THE CHAIRPERSON

The head of the FASAB is its Chairperson. Although the Board is responsible for establishing detailed operating procedures, the Chairperson, working with the Executive Director, directs FASAB operations. The Chairperson will:

   a) preside at meetings and hearings,
   b) confer with the Sponsors regarding the activities of the FASAB and its progress,
   c) consult with staff members regarding task forces,
   d) review the agenda for each meeting,
   e) request that the Executive Director provide lists of potential projects for consideration by the members of the FASAB as described at page 4,
   f) issue responses to requests and inquiries, and statements of policy,
   g) meet periodically and separately with each member to provide annual performance feedback to members,
   h) act on any reports of undue influence from a member,[6]
   i) convey the annual report (see page 18) to the Sponsors, Appointments Panel members, and the AICPA's president and director of governmental auditing and accounting,
   j) forward any notification by OMB or GAO of an additional 90-day review to the Appointments Panel members, and the AICPA's president and director of governmental auditing and accounting, and
   k) serve as Chairperson of the Appointments Panel and the Administrative Steering Committee.

The Chairperson may delegate or assign particular functions or duties to the FASAB staff, task forces, and such others as s/he may decide.

Following consultation with the Executive Director (or the Director's designee) and the Board, the Chairperson may establish and appoint individuals to FASAB task forces and other committees and groups. Before doing so, the Chairperson will consult with other FASAB members and the Executive Director. The FASAB's Chairperson, in consultation with the Executive Director and the Administrative Steering Committee, is also responsible for establishing operating and administrative procedures for task forces to the extent appropriate. The Chairperson has authority to approve a research project following consultation with the FASAB's Executive Director.

The Chairperson may invite an organization to name an individual to participate in meetings. The Chairperson will determine the extent of the participation and whether

---

[6] See the Statement of Member Responsibilities for guidance regarding a member's responsibility to raise any concerns regarding undue influence to the Chairperson.

it is ongoing or intermittent except that such participation may not include voting on any matter.

EXECUTIVE DIRECTOR

The FASAB's Executive Director shall be the Designated Federal Official (DFO) for purposes of the Federal Advisory Committee Act (FACA), and will work closely with the Chairperson to ensure compliance with FACA and implementing regulations promulgated by the General Services Administration (GSA). The Executive Director, or the Director's designee, in the role of DFO, shall approve the date, time, and place, and the agenda for each Board meeting, and shall attend each meeting. The Executive Director, or his or her designee on the FASAB staff, shall work closely with Treasury and OMB to ensure compliance with 41 C. F. R. §§102-3.115 and 102-3.120 and other applicable FACA requirements.

The Executive Director will administer annually:

1. the member evaluation process based on an evaluation form approved by at least a majority of the members and administered on a calendar year basis,
2. during the fourth quarter of each fiscal year, members will be asked to confirm their independence, adherence to the ethics policy, and that any undue influence experienced has been reported,[7]
3. during the fourth quarter of each fiscal year, a survey[8] of members to assess the Board's performance relative to the AICPA criteria for a standards-setting body, and
4. the process for preparing the annual report for each fiscal year (see page 17) to be approved by at least a majority of the Board.

ADMINISTRATIVE STEERING COMMITTEE

Mission. The mission of the Administrative Steering Committee (Steering Committee) is to ensure that the Board continues to meet its mission and conform with the criteria established by the AICPA for an entity designated as a source for GAAP. To that end, the Steering Committee assists the Sponsors in overseeing the administration of the Board, including its human and financial resources.

---

[7] The results will be conveyed to the Chairperson and members of the Appointments Panel.
[8] The survey results will be accumulated and summarized by FASAB staff or contractors under the direction of the Executive Director. With the exception of any sensitive personnel information, the survey data and the summary will be provided to the Board and the Appointments Panel, and included in the public records maintained by the Board.

Composition. The Steering Committee, comprising the GAO, OMB and Treasury Board members and the Chairperson of the FASAB, is an interagency committee of the Sponsors. The Chairperson of the FASAB will serve as the Chairperson of the Steering Committee.

Meetings. The Executive Director, after consultation with the Chairperson of the FASAB, shall schedule, convene, and attend meetings of the Steering Committee. The Steering Committee meetings will be announced in the *Federal Register* and will be open to public observation unless privileged or confidential information is being discussed. Privileged or confidential information may include internal personnel rules and practices, trade secrets, and financial information or personal information where disclosure would constitute a clearly unwarranted invasion of personal privacy.

Responsibilities. The Steering Committee is responsible for:
1. annually approving and recommending a budget to the Sponsors.
2. arranging for necessary reimbursable agreements among the Sponsors.
3. personnel matters such as:
a. providing input to the chairperson on the annual performance appraisal and expectation setting for the Executive Director, and
b. approving new professional staff hires recommended by the Executive Director.
4. supporting selection of new non-federal members through the Appointments Panel.
5. overseeing the annual member performance evaluation process.
6. approving final policies regarding member ethics, financial disclosure requirements, and Board procedures.
7. monitoring the Board's due process procedures.
8. serving as liaison between the Sponsors and the AICPA regarding the Board's status as the source of GAAP for federal reporting entities.
9. being familiar with the AICPA's criteria for GAAP standard-setting bodies and reportable events.
10. developing, as needed, any necessary remedial action plan following occurrence of a reportable event.

In support of the Steering Committee's communications with the AICPA, the Chairperson will maintain communications with the AICPA regarding the Board's continued conformance with the criteria established for GAAP standard-setting bodies and the Appointment Panel's adherence to its Policies and Procedures. At a minimum, the Chairperson will convey the annual report timely and notify, subject to any statutory limitations on the release of federal records, the AICPA of the occurrence of any reportable events within 60 days of receiving a report of an event. The Chairperson may consult with any appropriate committee (e.g., the Steering Committee or the Appointments Panel) prior to reporting the event. Such communications will be provided to the AICPA chairperson with copies to the

AICPA's president/CEO and director of governmental auditing and accounting. The Chairperson will coordinate with the AICPA regarding development of a remedial action plan by the Steering Committee as appropriate.

Budget Decisions. Unanimous agreement to the annual budget by the Treasury, OMB and GAO members is required for budget and funding decisions. Budgets will be reviewed by the end of May for each upcoming budget submission (e.g., the FY20X3 budget would be reviewed in May, 20X1). Reimbursable agreements normally are executed in the first quarter of each fiscal year.

Reportable Events. Reportable events are events indicative of potential non-conformance with the AICPAs Rule 203 criteria. Examples include but are not limited to:

1. The resignation or termination of a non-federal member
2. The resignation or termination of a federal member for other than a job change or retirement
3. A FASAB member notifies the Chairperson of undue influence (see the Statement of Members Responsibilities, Addendum 3, for additional information)
4. During the review period provided for statements, GAO or OMB, in accordance with the MOU, object to the statement and it is returned to the Board for further consideration
5. A Sponsor directs agencies to depart from generally accepted accounting principles
6. A Sponsor does not approve an Appointments Panel member recommendation

APPOINTMENTS PANEL

The Appointments Panel comprises not more than seven members, to include the FASAB Chairperson, a representative of the Financial Accounting Foundation, and two representatives of the AICPA as well as the FASAB members who represent Treasury, OMB and GAO. The panel is convened and chaired by the FASAB chairperson. The panel advises the Treasury, OMB and GAO on appointments and re-appointments of the six non-federal members and offers improvement recommendations as needed. The panel will meet, subject to the requirements of FACA, as needed (but at least annually) to:

1. consider nominations,
2. identify qualified individuals to be selected as candidates for appointment to the Board, and
3. consider related matters including criteria for candidates and improvement recommendations.

The panel will develop detailed operating procedures including guidance regarding their roles and responsibilities.

TECHNICAL STAFF

The Executive Director is responsible for determining the FASAB's personnel requirements and for selecting its staff.[9] The Executive Director, in consultation with the Administrative Steering Committee, has authority to hire, retain, and contract with staff members and to decide their remuneration, in accordance with policies of the U.S. Government Accountability Office, and to contract with any other persons or organizations for research and other technical services to be performed by consultants or independent contractors. The Executive Director shall decide their duties.

The FASAB may supplement its permanent technical staff through a "Fellow Program." Members of this program typically have experience in public accounting, academe, government, or industry. They serve as technical staff members on the understanding that they expect to return to their former employers after a period generally not in excess of 2 years on the FASAB's staff. Service as a FASAB fellow shall not affect a fellow's rights after leaving FASAB to publish utilizing knowledge or expertise gained during service with FASAB.

TASK FORCES

The Chairperson of the FASAB will establish a task force when he or she deems it appropriate. Before doing so, the Chairperson will consult with other FASAB members and the Executive Director regarding the composition of the task force as well as its purpose and expected duration. Task force members may be anyone possessing an expertise or viewpoint relevant to the project. The Chairperson of the FASAB will designate a task force Chairperson as needed (absent a designated Chairperson, FASAB staff will lead task force efforts). The FASAB's Chairperson, in consultation with the Executive Director and the Administrative Steering Committee, is also responsible for establishing operating and administrative procedures for task forces to the extent appropriate.

Task forces play an important role in the accounting standards-setting process by providing expertise and a diversity of viewpoints on a project. Task force members are encouraged to make oral presentations at the FASAB's meetings or public hearings, to submit comments and position papers, and to comment on exposure drafts and on such other matters as the FASAB may request.

---

[9]Selection of professional staff is subject to approval by the Administrative Steering Committee.

Although a task force may be appointed for any purpose related to the duties of the FASAB, a task force for an assigned project generally will be involved in advising, assisting, and consulting on the following:

1. The definition of the problem and the scope of the project;

2. The nature and extent of additional research, if any, that might be done, and by whom it might be performed; and

3. The preparation of a discussion memorandum, research reports, exposure draft or other document including appropriate federal accounting and financial reporting issues, and such summary and related documents as the FASAB may determine to be appropriate.

Task force members serve as volunteers and are not compensated. Travel expenses are generally not reimbursed. However, in the event that a task force member offers a unique perspective and attendance by teleconference is not sufficient the Executive Director may decide to reimburse task force members for necessary travel expenses.

RESEARCHERS FOR PRE-AGENDA ITEMS

In consultation with the Executive Director and the Board, the Chairperson of the FASAB may authorize researchers to conduct research projects as s/he may deem desirable. Research is to be conducted by the FASAB's technical staff, task forces, fellows, consultants, or independent contractors. The three Sponsors, the Executive Director, other members of the FASAB, or any other individual or organization may submit proposals for research to the Chairperson. Written research data and summaries of research data are a part of the FASAB's public files.

APPENDIX B: ANNUAL REPORT, NOTICES, MEETINGS, AND PUBLIC HEARINGS

ANNUAL REPORT

An annual report (supplementing information available through a Federal Advisory Committee Act (FACA) database administered by the General Services Administration's Committee Management Secretariat) will be provided by March 15th of each year. In addition to making the report publicly available, copies will be provided to the Sponsors, members of the Appointments Panel, and the AICPA President/CEO and director of governmental auditing and accounting. The annual report will provide information regarding:

1. activities of the Administrative Steering Committee and the Appointments Panel,
2. whether a review of the FASAB's governance documents, including the Rules of Procedure and the Policies and Procedures for the FASAB Appointments Panel, was performed by the Board, the Steering Committee, or the Appointments Panel during the year
   a. if so, whether any significant changes were made
   b. if not, the date that the last such review was performed
3. the results of an annual survey of members regarding performance relevant to the criteria established for a GAAP standard-setting body,
4. any issues identified through the annual confirmation that members were independent, adhered to the ethics policy, and that any undue influence experienced has been reported,
5. human and financial resources available during each of the past two years and anticipated for the coming year,
6. future opportunities and challenges including any suggestions for continuous improvement, and
7. the results of a self-assessment of trends in the annual performance results every fifth-year.

The Executive Director will administer the process for developing the annual report. The draft annual report will be provided to the members of the Appointments Panel for comment prior to its submission to the Board. The Appointments Panel members will be asked to provide any suggestions for continuous improvement based on their experiences and their review of the draft. Following input from the Appointments Panel, the draft annual report will be considered during a public meeting of the Board. The annual report will be issued electronically when approved by at least a majority of the members of the Board and will be unaudited. A press release will announce its availability.

NOTICES

The Executive Director of the FASAB is responsible for announcing developments relating to the operations and activities of the FASAB and for ensuring that all documents are available for public inspection as provided by FACA and the Freedom of Information Act (FOIA). All public announcements contemplated by these Rules of Procedure will be made by or at the direction of the Executive Director, or the Director's designee, as the Designated Federal Officer under FACA, in consultation with the Chairperson. The Executive Director will make public announcements in the *Federal Register*, in accordance with FACA, of the following:

1. Additions and other changes to the FASAB's agenda of projects;

2. The time, date, and place of each meeting of the FASAB, or committee created by the FASAB; the agenda for the meeting; the extent (if any) to which the meeting is to be closed to public observation and the reasons for closing it; and a telephone number to call for further information;

3. Organization of and appointments to task forces and task force assignments;

4. Issuance of discussion memorandums or other related documents, and background and other materials for public hearings;

5. Issuance of reports prepared by or for the FASAB or any of its task forces including written and research data and summaries of such data;

6. The FASAB's intention to convene public hearings and changes in the time, date, location, or general format of a hearing previously announced;

7. Issuance and availability of Statements of Federal Financial Accounting Standards, Interpretations, Technical Bulletins, Technical Releases, Staff Implementation Guidance, and Statements of Federal Financial Accounting Concepts; exposure drafts of proposed pronouncements; and other significant FASAB communications;

8. Completion of a significant phase of a project not otherwise publicly announced; and

9. Determinations by the FASAB to review or reexamine any effective Statement of Federal Financial Accounting Standards, Statement of Federal Financial Accounting Concepts, or other effective federal financial accounting principle.

Documents made available to or prepared for or by the Board are part of the public file of the FASAB. They are available for public inspection at the FASAB's offices to the extent provided for by FACA and FOIA. Examples of available documents are:

1. Operating and project plans of the FASAB;

2. Discussion memorandums or other related documents, and background and other materials for, and notices of, public hearings;

3. Outlines of proposed oral presentations at public hearings received by the FASAB, and transcripts of public hearings;

4. Reports prepared by or for the FASAB or any of its task forces, written research data and summaries of such data, and written comments and position papers received by the FASAB from FASAB task forces, members of them, and other individuals and organizations (other than proprietary material of a general character and statistical data and data requested by the FASAB, under confidential treatment as permitted by law);

5. Statements of Federal Financial Accounting Standards, Interpretations, Technical Releases, Statements of Federal Financial Accounting Concepts, exposure drafts, and other documents made available for public comment.

6. Other significant FASAB communications;

7. The ballots of members of the Federal Accounting Standards Advisory Board, and comments of dissenting members, on the issuance of Statements of Federal Financial Accounting Standards, Interpretations, and Statements of Federal Financial Accounting Concepts;

8. The minutes of meetings of the FASAB (subject to the limitations set forth in or contemplated by these rules);

9. Requests to address new issues or to review or reexamine effective Statements of Federal Financial Accounting Standards, Interpretations, Statements of Federal Accounting Concepts, or other effective federal financial accounting principle, and the responses to them;

10. The annual reports of the Chairperson of the FASAB about the FASAB's activities and its progress, the annual report of closed or partially closed meetings, and other reports and records retained pursuant to the requirements of FACA (see 41 CFR § 102-3.175).

The Executive Director shall determine, after consultation with the General Counsel, whether any FASAB record will be withheld from public release, and a record of such determination shall be kept in the FASAB public file.

MEETINGS

1. _Definition_. For purposes of this section, a "meeting" means the deliberations (with or without others present and in person or via electronic means) of the members of the FASAB, or of the members of a committee of the FASAB established by the Board, to conduct or dispose of official business of the Board. For this purpose, a meeting does not include informal discussion among FASAB members that involves simply the reporting of events or the consideration of facts that will not predetermine official Board actions. It does not include "administrative work," which is a meeting of two or more Board members or subcommittee or task force members convened solely to discuss administrative matters of FASAB or to receive administrative information from a federal officer or agency. Neither does it include an informal gathering primarily of a social nature.

2. _Frequency_. The Board will meet whenever the Chairperson deems necessary. A meeting will be called if at least a majority of the Board requests a meeting. Board members are expected to attend all meetings.

3. _Conduct of Meetings_. The Chairperson will preside at meetings and has discretion to determine whether set rules of order will be followed. The objectives are collegial interaction among members, clear direction or input to staff or others, and efficient and effective decision-making. Informal but orderly proceedings will normally best serve those objectives.

4. _Access_. Except as provided in these rules, and in accordance with the FACA, all meetings of the FASAB will be open to public observation. The Executive Director will assure that the meeting place is accessible to all interested parties.

To close all or a portion of a meeting the FASAB will submit a request to the Sponsors or the Sponsor's designee stating the specific provisions of the Government in the Sunshine Act, 5 U.S.C. Section 552b, which justify the closure. After the General Counsel reviews the request, the Sponsors or the Sponsor's designee shall issue a determination addressing whether all or part of the meeting shall be closed. The determination should be available to the public and, if the meeting is closed, should cite the specific exemption(s) used from the Government in the Sunshine Act. These exemptions include, among others, discussions that relate solely to the internal personnel rules and practices of an agency, and those that involve trade secrets and commercial or financial information obtained from a person and that are privileged or confidential. They also include information of a personal nature where disclosure would constitute a clearly unwarranted invasion of personal privacy, certain investigatory records and certain records related to regulation of financial institutions.

If a meeting is to be closed in whole or in part to public observation, then the FASAB will publish in the *Federal Register*, at least 15 days before the meeting, the reasons for closing the meeting (or portion thereof). The FASAB will repeat such announcement at its next meeting open in whole or in part to public observation.

5. <u>Notice</u>. At the approval of the Executive Director (acting as the DFO), the Board shall give 15-day advance notice in the *Federal Register* of the time, date, and place of each FASAB meeting. The notice will include the agenda for the meeting, the extent (if any) to which the meeting is to be closed to public observation and the reasons for closing it, and a telephone number to call for further information. In exceptional circumstances, the Board may give less than 15 days notice, if the reasons for doing so are included in the published notice of meeting. Any change in the time, date, or place of a meeting, and any determination to close a meeting previously announced as being open in whole or in part (and the reasons for closing it) or to open a meeting (or a portion thereof) previously announced as being closed, will be published in the *Federal Register*.

6. <u>Adjourning</u>. The Executive Director, as DFO and in consultation with the Chairperson, may adjourn any meeting in whole or in part to reconvene at another time, date, or place. The new meeting will be properly announced in the *Federal Register*. The Executive Director also shall use other methods to ensure that interested parties know about the meeting. These methods may include mailing written or electronic announcements to such individuals as the Chairperson or Executive Director may determine.

7. <u>Information</u>. Requests for information about FASAB meetings may be directed during normal business hours to the FASAB's Executive Director or FASAB. Those planning to attend a meeting are encouraged to contact by telephone the FASAB's Secretary shortly before the meeting date to confirm information about the meeting.

8. <u>Minutes</u>. In accordance with FACA, the FASAB will maintain minutes of its meetings that will summarize the matters discussed and the votes taken. They are a part of the FASAB's public file. The Executive Director shall ensure that the Chairperson certifies the accuracy of the minutes of all FASAB meetings, pursuant to FACA and the GSA's implementing regulations, 41 CFR § 102-3.165.

PUBLIC HEARINGS

The FASAB will seek information about federal accounting and related matters to prepare for its standard-setting meetings by convening a public hearing whenever, in the judgment of the FASAB, it is desirable to do so. The FASAB will decide based on majority views expressed through oral polling of members the number of public hearings to be held for a project. The Executive Director will coordinate the time, date, location, and general format of each public hearing. Generally, public hearings will be held in conjunction with a regularly scheduled meeting and conducted by the Chairperson. Quorum for a public hearing is at least a majority of the members. The Executive Director will attend each hearing.

Because a public hearing constitutes a meeting under FACA, FASAB will make information available and conduct the hearing in accordance with FACA. Generally the FASAB will publicly announce its intent to convene a public hearing at least 60 days before the earliest date of the hearing. A shorter period (not less than 30 days) may be used when considered appropriate by the FASAB. Such public announcements will be by the *Federal Register*. Each such notice of public hearing will set forth:

1. The time, date, location, and general format of the hearing;

2. A brief statement of the subject or purpose of the hearing;

3. The date or dates before the hearing by which those wishing to be heard at the hearing are to notify the FASAB and by which written comments, position papers, and outlines of oral presentations are to be received by the FASAB;

4. The extent to which a discussion memorandum, exposure draft, or other material is the basis for, or otherwise available in connection with, the hearing;

5. Procedures applicable to the hearing; and

6. Such other information as the FASAB may decide.

Any individual or organization may request to be heard at a public hearing. The FASAB will schedule all those making timely requests. Submission of written comments, a position paper, or an outline of proposed oral presentation is encouraged. Copies of these comments received by the FASAB will be distributed to members of the Board and are a part of its public file.

Public hearings may be adjourned, in whole or in part, to reconvene at another time, or location. They may be extended to additional date or dates at the same or different locations, with the same or a different format. There will be an announcement of the reconvening at the hearing and every effort will be made outside the hearing to notify interested parties of the change. All hearings will be held at a reasonable time to give the public an opportunity to attend. Hearings will be accessible to the public.

APPENDIX C: PUBLICATIONS

INTRODUCTION

In discharging its responsibilities the FASAB develops or causes to be developed various publications. The following chart presents the publications FASAB has used, how they are developed and due process requirements.

TYPES OF PUBLICATIONS	USE AND DEVELOPMENT	DUE PROCESS REQUIREMENTS[10]
PRELIMINARY DOCUMENTS:	Preliminary documents may not be followed immediately by issuance of a final pronouncement. An exposure draft precedes each final pronouncement.	
Research Reports (RR)	The Board may request an RR. Staff, a task force or others generally would develop the report. The report is used by the Board and others in considering accounting concepts and standards.	The Chairperson confers with the Board prior to issuance of an RR.
Discussion Memoranda (DM)	Staff, a task force or others may develop a DM. DMs define problems, identify issues (scope), present research findings, summarize relevant literature, and present alternative solutions. DMs request comments.	The Chairperson confers with the Board prior to issuance of a DM. The DM provides guidance for submission of comments including a deadline for comments. The anticipated comment period is 60 days and the minimum is 30 days. All comments are provided to the Board members with a staff (or task force) summary and analysis. The Board may convene a public hearing.
Invitations to Comment (ITC)	The Board may develop an ITC to invite comment on alternatives or proposals. An ITC may be presented in a wide variety of forms. For example, an ITC may solicit comments on a proposal made by another standard setting body or may present alternatives developed by the Board.	An ITC may only be issued if at least a majority of members voting approve its issuance. The ITC specifies a date (the anticipated comment period is 60 days and the minimum is 30 days) and instructions for submission of comments. All comments are provided to the Board members with a staff (or task force) summary and analysis. The Board may convene a public hearing.
Preliminary Views (PV)	The Board may develop a PV to solicit comment on a preliminary	A PV may only be issued if at least a majority of members approve its

---

[10] (Note that all publications are subject to *Federal Register* notice requirements. The requirements presented here are summarized.)

	view of at least a majority of the Board's members. Members are permitted to express alternative views.	issuance. The PV specifies a date (the anticipated comment period is 60 days and the minimum is 30 days.) and instructions for submission of comments. All comments are provided to the Board members with a staff (or task force) summary and analysis. The Board may convene a public hearing.
EXPOSURE DRAFTS (ED)	The Board must develop an ED to solicit comment on each proposal before issuing a final pronouncement. The ED presents the proposal in the form of a final pronouncement. Members may present alternative views. Contents of an ED are outlined in sections following this table.	An ED may only be issued if at least a majority of members approve its issuance. The ED specifies a date (the anticipated comment period is 90 days and the minimum is 30 days) and instructions for submission of comments. All comments are provided to the Board members with a staff (or task force) summary and analysis. The Board may convene a public hearing.
FINAL PRONOUNCEMENTS:		
Statements of Federal Financial Accounting Standards (SFFAS)	Statements establish authoritative accounting standards at the highest level in the GAAP hierarchy. Typically, a Statement includes definitions of terms, recognition, measurement, disclosure, supplementary information requirements and an effective date including transition guidance such as whether early implementation is permitted. Members may present dissents.	Following an affirmative vote by at least a two-thirds majority of the members, each SFFAS is submitted to the Secretary of the Treasury, the Director of OMB, and the Comptroller General. If, within 90 days after its submission, neither the Director of OMB nor the Comptroller General objects to the SFFAS, then it shall be published by FASAB. An additional 90 day review is possible if requested by Director of OMB or the Comptroller General. If there is an objection that, in accordance with the MOU, prevents its issuance then the Statement is returned to the Board for further consideration. An announcement of the outcome - either issuance or return to the Board - is published in the *Federal Register*. Per page 14, an objection is a reportable event. In addition, the CFO Act (Public Law No: 101-576) requires capital accounting standards to be reported to the Congress and that a period of 45 days of continuous session of the Congress be allowed for review prior to issuance
Interpretations	Interpretations clarify SFFAS provisions.	Following an affirmative vote by at least a majority of the members, Interpretations are submitted to the members representing Treasury,

		OMB, or GAO. If, within 45 days after its submission, none of these members object, then it shall be published by FASAB. If there is an objection that, in accordance with the MOU, prevents its issuance then the Statement is returned to the Board for further consideration. An announcement of the outcome - either issuance or return to the Board - is published in the *Federal Register*. Per page 14, an objection is a reportable event.
Statements of Federal Financial Accounting Concepts (SFFAC)	Statements on concepts are more general than statements of standards and do not contain specific recommendations that become authoritative requirements for federal agencies and auditors. Instead, statements on concepts provide general guidance to the Board itself as it deliberates on specific issues. They also help others to understand federal accounting and financial reports.	Following an affirmative vote by at least a two-thirds majority of the members, SFFAC are submitted to the Secretary of the Treasury, the Director of OMB, and the Comptroller General.. If, within 90 days after its submission, neither the Director of OMB nor the Comptroller General objects to the concepts, then it shall be announced in the *Federal Register* and published by FASAB. An additional 90 day review is possible if requested by Director of OMB or the Comptroller General. If there is an objection that, in accordance with the MOU, prevents its issuance then the Statement is returned to the Board for further consideration. An announcement of this action is published in the Federal Register. Per page 14, an objection is a reportable event. .
Technical Bulletins (TB)*	Technical Bulletins provide guidance for applying existing FASAB Statements and Interpretations and resolving accounting issues not directly addressed in them by establishing new standards.	Due process procedures, content specifications, and voting requirements are found in Technical Bulletin 2000-1. A Bulletin will not be issued if a majority of the FASAB members object either to the guidance in it or to communicating that guidance in a Technical Bulletin.
Technical Releases (TR)*	TRs provide guidance for applying existing Statements and Interpretations but may not promulgate new accounting standards.	The AAPC Charter and operating procedures specify due process procedures, AAPC voting requirements, and FASAB approval requirements. All proposed technical releases are ultimately submitted to the FASAB. If, within 45 days after submission, either at least a majority of the FASAB or a member representing Treasury, OMB or GAO

		objects to the proposed technical release, then it shall be returned to the AAPC for further consideration. If, within 45 days after its submission, neither at least a majority of FASAB nor a member representing Treasury, OMB or GAO objects to the proposed technical release, then it shall become final.
Staff Implementation Guidance (SIG)*	SIG provide guidance for applying existing Statements and Interpretations but may not promulgate new accounting standards.	The staff policy manual provides guidelines for the development of proposed implementation guidance. The executive director and the chairperson receive the draft SIG for review and must concur with any staff proposed guidance. This review is followed by a public meeting to discuss the proposal and a fifteen day public comment period. Following the comment period, a final SIG is prepared and provided to the full Board for a 15 day review period. If a majority of the Board does not object, the SIG is signed by the executive director and issued. (See the staff policy manual for additional information.)

*TBs, TRs, and SIG each may be used to provide implementation guidance. TBs may also be used to provide new standards. With that exception, the primary difference between these pronouncements is the due process requirements.

Preliminary documents may take a variety of forms. Thus, no content specifications have been developed. Content specifications follow for all other publications.

EXPOSURE DRAFTS

Publishing. Exposure drafts will be published electronically. Printed copies of the exposure draft will be mailed to all individuals and organizations that request printed copies. Exposure drafts, and notices of issuance of exposure drafts, will specify the time and manner in which individuals and organizations may comment. Written comments and position papers received in respect of exposure drafts are provided to all members and become a part of the FASAB's public file.

Notice. Notice of the availability of all exposure drafts will be made by *Federal Register* announcement, news release, and in the FASAB News.

Content. Exposure drafts include the same information as related final pronouncements with the exception of the number of Board members voting in favor and against the exposure draft (the "vote count"). The vote count is excluded because members sometimes may vote to issue a document so that comments will be solicited on their alternative view. In that case, the vote count would not be indicative of the support for the proposed solution.

Exposure drafts also include specific requests for comment. Respondents are encouraged to address the specific questions but also are invited to share their views concerning other issues relevant to the exposure draft.

If requested, "alternative views" will be incorporated in exposure drafts to request comments on the specific view or proposal of a member or a group of members that differs from the majority view of the Board. Members should draft their own alternative view but may seek assistance from the staff. Members are encouraged to seek input from individual members of the Board on draft alternative views. Generally, the alternative view should explain the alternative treatment, why the member believes this to be a more appropriate treatment than the treatment proposed by the majority of the Board, and pose specific questions to respondents. The alternative view should clearly state the difference(s) between the Board's proposal and the alternative proposal, and should not reiterate positions that the majority of the Board has taken.

To ensure that the views expressed in an alternative view are clearly distinguished from the majority view, the following standard text will precede the alternative view:

Individual members sometimes choose to express an alternative view when they disagree with the Board's majority position on one or more points in a proposed standard. The alternative view discusses the precise point or points of disagreement with the majority position and the reasons therefore. The ideas, opinions, and statements presented in the alternative view are those of the individual member alone. However, the individual member's view may contain general or other statements that may not conflict with the majority position, and in fact may be shared by other members. The material following was prepared by an individual member and is presented as an alternative view.

Draft alternative views should be provided to the Board for their consideration at the earliest possible point in deliberations. Every effort should be made to provide an alternative view for discussion at a public meeting of the Board in advance of balloting. If a member indicates a desire to express an alternative view but does not provide the written materials within four working days of the due date for the ballot on that ED, staff will include a statement in the exposure draft's basis for conclusions as follows:

Individual members sometimes choose to express an alternative view when they disagree with the Board's majority position on one or more points in a proposed standard. The alternative view discusses the precise point or points of disagreement with the majority position and the reasons therefore. The ideas, opinions, and statements presented in the alternative view are those of the individual member alone. However, the individual member's view may contain general or other statements that may not conflict with the majority position, and in fact may be shared by other members. A member indicated that an alternative view was desired but was unable to submit a written expression of those alternative views before the publication date of this exposure draft. Readers may contact the FASAB offices to request a copy of any alternative view provided by the member after the publication date of this exposure draft. In addition, any alternative view will be posted on the FASAB website when it becomes available (see www.fasab.gov/exposure.htm).

The Board provides more detailed guidance relating to the role of Board members through a Statement of Board Members Responsibilities.

FINAL PRONOUNCEMENTS

The Board will publish notice of issuance of each Statement of Federal Financial Accounting Standards, Statement of Federal Financial Accounting Concepts, Interpretation, Technical Bulletin, Technical Release, and Staff Implementation Guidance in the Federal Register. The Board will also publish notices of issuance of each preliminary document and exposure draft by Federal Register notice.

The following describes the content of each type of final pronouncement.

STATEMENTS OF FEDERAL FINANCIAL ACCOUNTING STANDARDS

Each Statement of Federal Financial Accounting Standards will include:

a. The standards of federal accounting;

b. The Statement's proposed effective date of application and method of transition;

c. Background information, including a brief summary of research results if a research project was undertaken concerning development of the exposure draft of the Statement or Statement;

d. The basis for the FASAB's conclusions, including its reasons (conceptual or otherwise) for accepting certain alternatives and rejecting others, and a summary of the more significant and relevant points of view communicated to the FASAB at public hearings and in written comments and position papers;

e. The number of Board members who voted in favor of the Statement and the number of those who voted against it or who abstained, if any. There shall also be a statement that the written ballots are available for public inspection at the FASAB's offices. Written dissents provided by individual members and the identity of the member;

     f. the authoritative status of any appendices shall be indicated; and

     g. Such other information as the FASAB may determine to be useful.

INTERPRETATIONS

Each Interpretation will include:

a. The interpretation of federal accounting standards or concepts;

b. The Statement's effective date of application and method of transition;

c. Background information;

d. The basis for the FASAB's conclusions; and

e. the authoritative status of any appendices shall be indicated;

     f. Written dissents provided by individual members and the identity of the member.

Interpretations approved by at least a majority of the Board members and not objected to by a member representing a Principal will be published by FASAB and announced in the Federal Register.

STATEMENTS OF FEDERAL FINANCIAL ACCOUNTING CONCEPTS

Statements of Federal Financial Accounting Concepts set forth fundamental ideas on which federal accounting standards will be based. More specifically, Statements of Federal Financial Accounting Concepts explain the objectives and ideas that the FASAB will use in developing standards of federal accounting. Statements of Concepts also enhance the ability of users to understand the content and limitations of information provided by federal accounting and financial reporting, and thus increase their ability to use that information effectively.

Each Statement of Federal Financial Accounting Concepts will include:

a. A preamble explaining the nature of concepts and their standing in the GAAP hierarchy;

b. The federal accounting concepts;

c. Background information, including a brief summary of research results if a research project was undertaken in connection with development of the Statement or exposure draft of Statement;

d. The basis for the FASAB's conclusions, including its reasons (conceptual or otherwise) for accepting certain alternatives and rejecting others, and a summary of the more significant and relevant points of view communicated to the FASAB at public hearings and in written comments and position papers;;

e. The number of Board members who voted in favor of the Statement and the number of those who voted against it or who abstained, if any. There shall also be a statement that the written ballots are available for public inspection at the FASAB offices.

f. Written dissents provided by individual members.

g. Such other information as the FASAB may determine to be useful.

TECHNICAL BULLETINS

FASAB Technical Bulletins provide guidance for applying FASAB Statements and Interpretations and resolving accounting issues not directly addressed by them. The following kinds of guidance may be provided in a Technical Bulletin:

a. Guidance to clarify, explain, or elaborate on an underlying Statement or Interpretation,

b. Guidance to address areas not directly covered by existing Statements or Interpretations,

c. Interim guidance on problems in applying an existing Statement or Interpretation currently under study by the FASAB, or

d. If applicable, guidance for applying FASB or GASB standards to federal activities. (See Technical Bulletin 2000-1 for guidelines for issuance of Technical Bulletins.)

Technical Bulletins will include an introduction, effective date, technical guidance, and a basis for conclusions.

TECHNICAL RELEASES

Technical Releases will be promulgated through a permanent committee, the Accounting and Auditing Policy Committee (AAPC). The AAPC has a separate Charter and Operating Procedures Techncial Releases will include an introduction, effective date, technical guidance, and a basis for conclusions.

STAFF IMPLEMENTATION GUIDANCE

Staff Implementation Guidance (SIG) will be developed as needed and is limited to guidance related to existing accounting standards. SIGs will include an introduction, effective date, technical guidance, and a basis for conclusions.

OTHER COMMUNICATIONS

The FASAB may, at its discretion and with or without appointment of task forces, research, notice, public hearings, or public exposure, issue in its name or at its direction other communications of an informational nature related to federal accounting and financial reporting, including the FASAB's mission, policies, and activities. Such communications may include, among others, discussion memorandums, summary and related documents, research reports, responses to requests and inquiries, and statements of policy dealing with matters of federal accounting and financial reporting.

AVAILABILITY OF PUBLICATIONS

To promote broad public participation in establishing and improving federal accounting standards, the FASAB will make available on request, without charge, at least one copy of each document made available for public comment. Information about the number of copies available without charge in any specific case, and the copies themselves, may be obtained by contacting the FASAB executive assistant at the FASAB offices or fasab@fasab.gov. The FASAB will maintain an electronic and/or written public communication process to enable users ready and free access to its publications including its newsletter.

APPENDIX D: MEDIA RELATIONS POLICY

Actions of the FASAB have an impact on many organizations within the Board's large and diverse constituency. The Board's constituency includes citizens and other users of information as well as preparers, auditors, political appointees and elected officials. Each of these constituencies perceives federal financial reporting from a different vantage point. The Rules of Procedure require extensive due process that is open to public observation and participation. In some cases, FASAB may garner attention from the news media.

Contact with the news media is important to the Board's communications efforts. Even a short news story will reach thousands more constituents than can be reached by other means. Thus, every effort should be made to help the reporter understand the subject matter, with the objective being accurate reporting.

POLICY OBJECTIVE: Accurate Reporting that Facilitates Due Process

The role of staff is to ensure that the technical points are understood by the reporter and to help potential respondents approach each proposal with an open mind. As staff, our objective is to solicit informed but unbiased responses from our constituents. Therefore, staff should not offer opinions on the possible policy impacts of proposals, describe the relative significance or weight of alternative proposals supported by members, draw analogies to other circumstances or existing standards in other domains (unless the analogies were discussed by members and support the majority conclusion or are otherwise non-controversial), or discuss the opinions or possible motivations of our members. Staff perspectives on these matters would carry great weight with constituents and may cause them to approach the issue with a less than open mind. Technical points include questions about what the current standards require, how those requirements would change under the Board's proposal or alternatives under consideration, and the process to be followed in changing accounting standards.

The role of members is to explain their point of view. Members should clarify that the views expressed are their own and that the Board's views are expressed in the published document.

In all cases, reporters should be encouraged to include information about the request for comment such as (1) how to access the proposal on the website and (2) the deadline for submitting comments.

GUIDELINES FOR MEMBERS AND STAFF:

Every effort also should be made to get out the Board's message when talking with a reporter. Even though he or she may have initiated the contact, please take the opportunity to spread the word. Important message points are included below.

Dealing with the media effectively is a learned skill. As a general rule, Board and staff members should participate in media training before talking with reporters. Media training is available from GAO's Learning Center. For the most part, only Board members, the Executive Director, or the specific Assistant Director responsible for the area of interest should respond to media inquiries.

The nature of the media inquiry will determine who should be answering the reporter's questions. A Board member should respond if the questions are policy oriented or if the reporter wants to understand a specific Board member's views. If the reporter is interested in the technical details of a project, the Assistant Director on the project should respond. Regardless of who responds to the inquiry, the individual should relate only what they believe the reporter could have learned by attending a meeting or reading a public document.

Calls from reporters unfamiliar with the Board, inquiring about something that is not the subject of a technical project, or where staff is uncertain about the guidelines should be referred to the Executive Director. The Executive Director answers general questions or refers the call to the appropriate person.

The Executive Director must be informed, orally or by e-mail, of any contact with the media on the day of such contact. The Executive Director will be responsible for alerting members and staff of impending news coverage. Ideally, members address questions regarding the underlying reasons for their views and, if they wish, any policy ramifications of proposals. In some cases, members do not wish to speak to the press. When a reporter should or wishes to speak with a member, staff should (1) take the reporter's contact information including organization, (2) determine the timeline the reporter is operating under, and (3) pass this information on to the member(s). The members will then return calls from reporters at their discretion.

Important Message Points

Accounting and financial reporting standards are essential for public accountability and for an efficient and effective functioning of our democratic system of government. Thus, federal accounting standards and financial reporting play a major role in fulfilling the government's duty to be publicly accountable and can be used to assess:

(1) the government's accountability and its efficiency and effectiveness, and
(2) the economic, political, and social consequences of the allocation and various uses of federal resources.

The FASAB issues federal accounting standards after following a due process consistent with the Memorandum of Understanding under which it operates. Due process includes consideration of the financial and budgetary information needs of citizens, congressional oversight groups, executive agencies, and the needs of other users of federal financial information.

.

APPENDIX E: MEMBER OR STAFF AUTHORED PUBLICATIONS AND PUBLIC SPEAKING

Members and staff are encouraged to publish articles related to Board activities, and to speak at meetings, conferences or other events. Policies regarding such activities are provided below.

(1) Disclaimer. All material prepared or presented by an individual member should include an appropriate disclaimer. Sample disclaimers include:

(a) The information contained in this article is the unofficial view of one of the FASAB members. Official positions of the FASAB are determined only after extensive due process and deliberations.

(b) The views expressed are those of the speaker. The Board expresses its views only in official publications.

(c) The views expressed in this article are those of the author, not of the FASAB. Official positions of the FASAB are determined only after extensive due process and deliberations.

(2) Travel Reimbursement.

(a) Non-federal members may accept reimbursement for travel costs and may make arrangements directly with sponsors.

(b) Staff may be authorized to accept on FASAB's behalf reimbursement for travel related to attendance at meetings or similar functions from non-Federal sources. Reimbursement may generally not be accepted for meetings, etc. that are required to carry out FASAB's duties, such as research regarding an active project. For example, staff cannot personally accept reimbursement to appear on a panel at a conference, but staff may ask FASAB to authorize staff's acceptance on FASAB's behalf. Note, however, that FASAB will not accept reimbursement from any source that has obtained, or is seeking to obtain business or financial relations with FASAB, seeks official action from FASAB, or has interests that may be substantially affected by the performance of staff's official duties. Staff may not solicit a third party for the payment of travel expenses for official duty.

(3) Conference Registration. Speakers may accept free attendance at a conference, seminar, or other event when they are a speaker or panel participant.

(4) Compensation. Members and staff may not receive compensation from any source other than the government for outside speaking or

writing that relate to their official duties. "Compensation" is the actual or constructive receipt of any benefit, including a donation to your favorite charity. It does NOT include reimbursements of travel expenses necessary to an approved outside speaking or writing engagement. The restriction applies whether the individual is on official duty, annual leave or in a nonpay status.

(5) <u>Gifts</u>. FASAB members and staff who appear as a speaker or panelist may accept modest noncash commemorative gifts from the sponsoring organization. They may not accept cash, gift certificates, or gift cards.

www.ingramcontent.com/pod-product-compliance
Lightning Source LLC
Chambersburg PA
CBHW052022280526
45793CB00005B/1091